AMERICA'S SUPERNATURAL SECRETS™

MONSTERS, BEASTS, AND DEMONS IN AMERICA

Kristi Lew

rosen publishing's
rosen
central

NEW YORK

Published in 2012 by The Rosen Publishing Group, Inc.
29 East 21st Street, New York, NY 10010

Library of Congress Cataloging-in-Publication Data

Lew, Kristi.
Monsters, beasts, and demons in America/Kristi Lew.—1st ed.
     p. cm.—(America's supernatural secrets)
Includes bibliographical references (p.   ) and index.
ISBN 978-1-4488-5532-2 (library binding)—
ISBN 978-1-4488-5584-1 (pbk.)—
ISBN 978-1-4488-5585-8 (6-pack)
1. Monsters—United States—Juvenile literature. I. Title.
QL89.L44 2012
001.944—dc23

                                                                            2011020641

Manufactured in the United States of America

CPSIA Compliance Information: Batch #W12YA: For further information, contact Rosen Publishing, New York, New York, at 1-800-237-9932.

Contents

Introduction

America can be a strange place. For example, some areas of the country seem to have more than their fair share of haunted houses. Other places seem to be favorite vacation spots for visitors from outer space. Still other locations are stalked by beings that are not necessarily human—beings with big teeth, long hair, and a funky smell. (All right, maybe that last part could describe some people.) But what about beasts with glowing red eyes, horns, and wings? Have you seen anything like that hanging around the neighborhood lately? Depending on where you live, maybe you have. Or maybe you will.

Tales of monsters, beasts, and demons make up many local legends. In some regions of the United States, these legends have been passed down from generation to generation. In other areas of the country, ones with more recent beastly sightings, these legends are still being written. Some mysterious monsters have been seen only in a particular town. Other beasts seem to travel and have been reported in many places around the country, where they are often given different names.

Are these legendary monsters real? Or are they the creation of some very active imaginations? That's hard to say. Evidence has shown that some of these unknown creatures were the products of practical jokes. Some have been explained as real animals that were mistaken for something strange. But the veracity of others is still a big question in many people's minds.

To answer those questions, people called cryptozoologists actively investigate these legendary animals, trying to gather evidence of their existence.

The Idaho Museum of Natural History displays a collection of plaster casts of Bigfoot prints. Were these gigantic footprints really made by a super-sized beast, or are they fakes?

Cryptozoologists call the creatures they seek "cryptids." Cryptids are not recognized by science as being real. At least, they aren't yet.

What are some of America's cryptids? Well, that depends on where you live. Different places have different environments and cultures. Therefore, they tend to host a variety of weird creatures. Let's travel America and meet some of these bizarre beasts. Our first stop is Bigfoot country.

Chapter 1
Tall, Dark, and Hairy

Bigfoot is probably the best-known legendary creature in America. In the United States, stories of this giant, hairy, apelike beast originated in the Pacific Northwest, specifically in northern California.

Bigfoot Gets a Name

Early one morning in 1958, a construction crew carving a new road in the California wilderness discovered a set of enormous footprints around one of their bulldozers. What could have possibly made these gigantic, humanlike footprints? Jerry Crew, the bulldozer's operator, made plaster casts of the 16-inch (41-centimeter) footprints and took them to the office of the local newspaper. Newspaper columnist Andrew Genzoli labeled the massive beast "Bigfoot." The name stuck.

What could be more frightening than knowing that a monster with huge feet might be skulking around camp while you sleep? How about running smack into the beast? That is exactly what happened one cold February night in 1962, according to California logger Robert Hatfield. While visiting his sister on the coast, Hatfield was awake late one night when he heard the family's dogs going crazy outside. Afraid that the dogs would wake his sister and brother-in-law, Hatfield stepped out of the house to calm them. That is when he saw it—a huge creature with a hairy head, shoulders, and chest, towering over the 6-foot (1.8-meter) backyard fence.

This still photograph from a 1977 film made by Ivan Marx supposedly shows the legendary Bigfoot walking in the California mountains. Is it really a picture of the massive, apelike beast?

Rightfully concerned, Hatfield returned to the house to wake his brother-in-law, Bud Jenkins. While Jenkins got his rifle, Hatfield stepped back outside. There was a horrible stink in the air, but the beast was nowhere to be seen. Hatfield decided to check around the property to make sure the monster was really gone. He rounded the corner of the house and ran right into the beast!

Truly scared now, Hatfield ran back to the house. The monster was right on his heels. Hatfield finally made it to the door and bolted inside. But the monster would not let him close the door. Holding the rifle, Jenkins yelled for Hatfield to let the big furry thing inside. He planned to shoot it, but he never got the chance. The huge hairy creature turned and ran away. Later, the police found an 11.5-inch (29-cm) muddy handprint on the door.

Five years after Robert Hatfield's run-in with Bigfoot, Roger Patterson and Bob Gimlin caught the beast on film in the Six Rivers National Forest in northern California. In what is possibly the most famous piece of Bigfoot evidence to date, the film appears to show a female Bigfoot walking toward the safety of the trees. For many years, people have debated the truth of the Patterson-Gimlin film. Does it actually contain images of the elusive Bigfoot? Or is it just a film of a tall guy in a gorilla suit?

A Bigfoot by Any Other Name

California is not the only place where people have seen hairy, humanlike creatures. These bipedal hominids exist in the folklore of cultures all over the world. Living on the edges of civilization, these sometimes giant, sometimes man-sized beasts are called wildmen. The hairy wildman of Australia is called the Yowie. In the snowy wilderness of the Himalayas, people say there is a white-furred wildman called the Yeti—also called the Abominable Snowman. In Canada, Bigfoot is known as Sasquatch. The Mayan, English, and Chinese cultures all have their own versions of the wildman, too.

In 1967, Bob Gimlin and Roger Patterson reported seeing a female Bigfoot in the woods of northern California. The two men claimed they filmed the beast and made these plaster casts of her footprints.

Even Americans outside of California have different names for the big, hairy bipeds inhabiting their states. Illinois, for example, has its own version of the hairy monster. First reported on a hot summer night in 1973, this beast is called the Murphysboro Mud Monster. Near midnight one evening, a young couple parked on a remote country road near the town's old boat ramp. Soon they heard a shriek that sounded like a very large, incredibly loud eagle. The couple reported seeing an 8-foot (2.4-m) white-haired beast covered in mud. When the police went to investigate, they found several footprints that were 10 to 12 inches (25.4 to 30.5 cm) long and 3 inches (7.6 cm) wide. Several

Large, hairy apes from the genus *Gigantopithecus* inhabited Earth about five hundred thousand years ago. Cryptozoologists have suggested that Bigfoot may be a relative of *Gigantopithecus* that somehow survived extinction.

police officers also reported hearing the terrifying shrieking. Is the Murphysboro Mud Monster an albino relative of Bigfoot? Or is it the same creature that was spotted in northern California, mistakenly identified as having white fur? No one knows.

People in the southern United States have seen Bigfoot-like creatures, too. Folks around Fouke, Arkansas, describe a 7-foot (2.1-m) dark, hairy creature they call the Southern Sasquatch. Another large, hairy cryptid reportedly lives

Why Are We So Interested in the Supernatural?

Since the beginning of humankind, people have sought explanations for the unknown. Brian Cronk, a psychology professor at Missouri Western State University, told MSNBC, "The human brain is always trying to determine why things happen, and when the reason is not clear, we tend to make up some pretty bizarre explanations."

For example, at one time people could not explain scientifically why the sun rose and set every day. They came up with an explanation anyway. According to Greek mythology, each day Apollo pulls the sun across the sky with his chariot.

What does Bigfoot help people understand? It is possible that Bigfoot is a stand-in for strange and frightening people. He could serve as a bogeyman, a creature used by adults to frighten children into behaving (and not going outside alone at night). Another explanation might be that the supernatural is just downright fun to think about. After all, lots of people love a mystery. The thought of a big, scary monster waiting for you in the wilderness sends chills down the spine. Thrills and chills are fun as long as they occur in the safety of our imaginations.

in the Florida Everglades. It is called the Skunk Ape because of its characteristically foul stench. The swamps of Louisiana hide a smelly Bigfoot called the Louisiana Wookie. No matter where they are found or what they are called, these wildmen all have one thing in common—they prefer wild, remote, uninhabited areas where they can easily disappear.

Is Bigfoot Real?

In 2002, the family of Ray Wallace, the leader of the road crew that found the first set of Bigfoot prints in 1958, reported that he had made it all up. According to Wallace's family, he had a friend carve 16-inch (41-cm) wooden feet. He strapped these feet to his boots and stomped around in the mud, creating the myth of Bigfoot. Many Bigfoot hunters, however, remain unconvinced. They assert that a human could not create the depth and the stride (distance between steps) shown in the prints.

In 2008, two Georgia men claimed to have found Bigfoot's body in the mountains of northern Georgia. They documented their startling discovery with pictures and handed DNA evidence over to scientists. It did not take long for DNA testing to prove the men's stories suspect. One of the samples proved to be human in origin. The other was opossum DNA. It turned out that the men were making a living running a Bigfoot expedition (tour) service. Both stood to profit from convincing people that the beast was real.

Believers explain away the DNA evidence by saying it must have been contaminated. Is Bigfoot real, or is it just some elaborate hoax? It's hard to say.

Big, apelike creatures may sound weird, but giant apes did roam the planet at one time. One ape, called *Gigantopithecus*, stood about 10 feet (3 m) tall and probably went extinct about three hundred thousand years ago. Could Bigfoot be a *Gigantopithecus* or another ancient animal that escaped extinction? It is extremely unlikely, scientists say. But it is possible, believers counter.

Chapter 2

Aquatic Anomalies

While some parts of America are covered in trees and swamps—just right for Bigfoot and his relatives to lurk in—other areas are covered in water. These environments give rise to sightings of another legendary animal—the sea serpent.

Monsters of the Deep

On a spit of land in the northeastern corner of Massachusetts sits America's oldest seaport, Gloucester. The area, called Cape Ann, juts out into the Atlantic Ocean and has a long, rich maritime history. It is also the site of some of America's oldest cryptid sightings. First reported in 1638 by an English traveler and author, John Josselyn, the Gloucester Sea Serpent is described as an enormous, snakelike beast.

Over the next 180 years, a small number of people reported seeing an 80- to 100-foot (24.4- to 30.5-m) monster lurking in the waters off the coast. Then, in 1817, the monster reared its horned, horse-sized head in earnest. In all, there would be eighteen sightings of the creature near Gloucester that year. There were so many sightings that a natural history organization called the Linnaean Society of New England was inspired to investigate. After collecting eyewitness accounts, members of the society determined that the creature was a previously unknown animal. They named it *Scoliophis atlanticus*.

This artwork depicts the Gloucester Sea Serpent as it was described in eye-witness accounts.

The serpent remained in the Gloucester area for much of the nineteenth century. In fact, in April 1859, a British sailing ship, *Banner*, was allegedly attacked by the creature. In total, approximately 190 sightings were reported by the end of the century. During the twentieth century, however, reports of the beast tapered off. There were only about fifty-six sightings, most of them before 1950. What happened to the Gloucester Sea Serpent?

Maybe the beast prefers warmer water. In 1936, the crew of a military helicopter reported seeing an unknown reptile swimming in the Chesapeake Bay, more than 400 miles (643.7 kilometers) south of Gloucester. The Chesapeake Bay is connected to the Atlantic Ocean, but it is surrounded on three sides by land—parts of Maryland and Virginia. Reported to be about 30 feet (9.1 m) long, as thick as a telephone pole, and dark in color, this snakelike

This photograph purportedly shows the Loch Ness monster, Nessie, in a Scottish lake.

monster was nicknamed Chessie. (The nickname is a nod to the world-famous Loch Ness monster, Nessie, which is said to inhabit Loch Ness, a lake in Scotland.) More recent evidence of Chessie includes a 1982 video. It appears to show the humped, snakelike creature off the shores of Kent Island, Maryland.

Today, you can see what Chessie looks like by taking a trip to Baltimore, Maryland, which lies close to the northernmost tip of the Chesapeake Bay. In Baltimore's Inner Harbor, tourists can rent paddleboats shaped like the legendary monster.

A Case of Mistaken Identity

Most scientists believe that most cryptids are really just cases of mistaken identity. For example, David Davies, a biologist from the Ohio Division of Wildlife, speculates that Bessie, Lake Erie's "monster," is most likely a lake sturgeon. These real-life fish can really be monstrous. They grow up to 7 feet (2.1 m) long, weigh more than 300 pounds (136.1 kilograms), and live to be 150 years old. Although the sturgeon is a bottom feeder, eating material at the bottom of the lake, it does occasionally come to the surface. When this happens, Davies believes that the sturgeon's tail could be mistaken for the neck of the Lake Erie monster.

In April 2009, the History Channel show MonsterQuest reported finding a new sea serpent with a trident-shaped tail in Florida. However, by early 2010, Florida Fish and Wildlife biologists announced that they had figured out the mystery. The so-called serpent was not an unknown sea creature, said the biologists. It was a manatee. Manatees are large, slow-moving marine mammals. Because they cannot move quickly, they are often injured when the propellers on motorboat engines hit them. The most likely cause of the unusual water pattern shown on MonsterQuest was a manatee with an injured tail—a tail that was split into three parts.

Freshwater Frights

In addition to its oceans, America has other fertile territories for water weirdness. The Great Lakes, located in the northeastern United States along the Canadian border, are the largest group of freshwater lakes on Earth. The shallowest and southernmost Great Lake, Lake Erie, is home to a creature known as Bessie. First spotted in Lake Erie's South Bay in 1898, this 30- to 40-foot (9.1- to 12.2-m) water serpent is said to be able to survive in the lake or on land.

Another water-dwelling creature vying for the title of "America's Loch Ness Monster" lives in Lake Champlain. Lake Champlain is a deep, freshwater lake bordered by New York, Vermont, and Quebec, Canada. Like the Gloucester Sea Serpent, Lake Champlain's monster, nicknamed "Champ," is reported to have a horse-shaped head with two small horns. Some people

Plesiosaurs were large marine reptiles that lived during the Jurassic period. Is it possible that a plesiosaur survived extinction and dwells in Lake Erie?

who have seen the beast say he looks like a plesiosaur, a prehistoric marine reptile that lived from 220 to 65.5 million years ago. Is it possible that a lone plesiosaur somehow survived the extinction of its fellow dinosaurs? If so, it would also have had to adapt to living in freshwater.

A giant freshwater octopus is purportedly living in a lake in Oklahoma (Lake Thunderbird, Lake Oolagah, or Lake Tenkiller, depending on who is telling the story). According to local legend, a horse-sized, aquatic beast with long tentacles and reddish-brown leathery skin attacks and kills unsuspecting swimmers. Believers say this accounts for the large number of unexplained drowning deaths that occur in the lake every year.

In fact, an animal similar to the Oklahoma octopus does exist in nature. The giant Pacific octopus is an intelligent creature that has reddish-brown skin. It can grow up to 600 pounds (272.2 kg)—although most top out at 50 to 90 pounds (22.7 to 40.8 kg)—and it has a beak that it uses to kill and pick apart prey. However, these gigantic beasts live only in the Pacific Ocean—as far as scientists know.

Chapter 3

Mysterious Monsters

Not all denizens of the deep stay in the water where they belong. Others wander about on land at will, disappearing into the deep only when they have been spotted.

Fearsome Frogs

The Ohio River is a large waterway that makes up the southern border of Ohio, Indiana, and Illinois. At 981 miles (1,578.8 km) long, the Ohio pours more water into the Mississippi River than any of its other tributaries. But water may not be the only thing the Ohio is contributing to the Mississippi. According to some reports, there are mysterious monsters that live in these waters.

Early one morning in May 1955, a businessman was traveling on a desolate stretch of country highway just outside of Loveland. The man said he saw three lizardlike, bipedal creatures standing by the side of the road. He described the beasts as being about 3 to 4 feet (.9 to 1.2 m) tall, with leathery skin, webbed hands and feet, and frog's heads on human bodies. Because of the proximity to the town of Loveland, the creatures became known as the Loveland Frogmen.

Later that year, a similar creature was reported farther downstream in Evansville, Indiana. Unlike the Loveland Frogmen, the Indiana beast turned out to be aggressive. One hot August day, Mrs. Darwin Johnson decided to go swimming in the Ohio River with a friend. While her friend lounged on the beach, Johnson paddled around in the shallows. She said she was grabbed around the knees and pulled underwater. She surfaced long enough to scream and alert her friend. However, she was quickly gripped from behind and pulled under again. Luckily, Johnson managed to escape the creature's hold and get away. Back on the beach, Johnson and her friend discovered several scratches and a green, palm-shaped handprint on Johnson's leg. It would be days before the green palm print faded. Because of the stain and scratches on Johnson's leg, the creature became known as the Green Clawed Beast. By comparison, the Loveland Frogmen seem positively passive and shy.

In fact, the Frogmen would not be seen for seventeen more years. Then, one cold March morning in 1972, one of the creatures darted out in front of a police officer who was carefully driving down the icy road in his cruiser. The officer slammed on his brakes to avoid hitting the beast, capturing the animal in his headlights. The creature stood up on its hind legs and looked at the policeman before scrambling over a guardrail and into the Little Miami River, a tributary of the Ohio River. Later that

Swamp creatures have been reported in many places in America, where they have been given different names. Whatever they are called, giant, man-shaped lizards would be quite frightening.

same year, a farmer with fields bordering the Ohio River also reported seeing four of the reptilian creatures on the riverbank.

Scaly and Scary

The Loveland Frogmen and the Green Clawed Beast are not the only bipedal water-dwellers among us. People have reported seeing half-human, half-reptilian creatures skulking around the remote swamps of America. One of these monsters, the Lizard Man, inhabits the Scape Ore Swamp in Lee County, South Carolina.

The first reported sighting of Lee County's Lizard Man occurred in 1988, when sixteen-year-old Christopher Davis stopped on a road near the swamp to change a flat tire. As he was finishing up, Davis reported hearing a sound behind him. When he turned around, he saw a 7-foot (2.1-m) man-shaped lizard with scaly green skin and glowing red eyes running toward him. Terrified, Davis jumped into his car and slammed the door. According to Davis, at this point the Lizard Man jumped on top of his car and clung to the roof. Davis drove off, swerving from side to side in an effort to shake off the beast. He managed to lose the creature somewhere along the way, but his car was badly damaged with deep scratches on the roof.

Other people who have seen South Carolina's Lizard Man reported that his three-toed hands and feet sport circular pads, allowing him to cling to objects, such as trees and cars, like a gecko. In the months following Davis's encounter with the beast, numerous people reported damage to cars parked near the swamp. Eventually, police in the area determined that the damage was most likely the work of a bear, not a Lizard Man.

Not to be outdone by South Carolinians, Florida residents claim to have their own hybrid reptile known as the Gatorman. Gatormen are said to inhabit the Florida Everglades along with the Skunk Ape. Reports of these half-human, half-alligator creatures date back to the early 1700s. Gatormen are said to have razor-sharp teeth in a human head, a child-sized torso, and the muscular tail of an alligator. With an overall length of approximately 5 feet (1.5 m), this creature is one you would definitely not want to encounter in the remote back swamps.

Charles Hoy Fort: Collector of Unexplained Mysteries

The terms "Fortean" and "Forteana" are often used to describe unusual phenomena. These terms originated with an American writer and paranormal researcher named Charles Hoy Fort. Born in New York in 1847, Fort spent much of his adult life collecting bizarre tales of UFO sightings, ghosts, and unknown creatures. Although he was once a news reporter, Fort did not seem to be overly concerned with whether the stories he collected and published were true or not. In 1929, Fort became good friends with a young novelist named Tiffany Thayer. Inspired by Fort's ideas and endeavors, Thayer founded the Fortean Society in 1931. The novelist Theodore Dreiser served as its first president. Although the Fortean Society ended when Thayer died in 1959, Fort's name remains synonymous with the bizarre, supernatural tales he collected.

Charles Fort collected supernatural tales on cards and scraps of paper. Upon his death, more than sixty thousand of his notes were donated to the New York Public Library.

The Montauk Monster

The Loveland Frogmen, the Lizard Man, and the Gatormen have only been encountered in remote, unpopulated areas. However, bizarre beasts occasionally wash up on the very populated shores of Long Island, New York. In 2008, for example, the remains of a mysterious creature washed up on a Montauk beach. The first picture of the unknown beast hit the Internet on July 13, showing what appeared to be a hairless dog with reddish-purple skin and a beak.

Speculation about the strange beast quickly spread across the Web. Was it a sea turtle without its shell? An escapee from the government's animal disease research facility on Plum Island? A sea monster? Finally, scientists weighed in and declared that, alas, it was

When a hairy beast with a bald head was dragged from an Ontario lake in 2010, people labeled it the "new Montauk Monster."

no monster after all. The creature was nothing more than a dead raccoon that had started to decompose in the surf. What about the fact that it had a beak? Biologists explained that the structure that looked like a beak was actually the raccoon's snout without the flesh that normally surrounds it.

Chapter 4

Winged Wonders

If cryptids really do exist, they certainly are shy. Although there have been hundreds of eyewitness accounts of these creatures, there is little physical evidence of their existence. The few photographs and videotapes that are purported to capture these beasts on film are of poor quality. In addition, the images are invariably taken from far away. This actually makes sense. Who wants to get close to a monster—on purpose? However, it makes it very difficult to determine what the images are really showing.

Getting photographs of cryptids is hard enough when the creatures poke their heads out of the water or peer around a tree in the woods. Capturing these unknown beasts on film gets even harder when they take to the sky.

Winged and Wicked

The New Jersey Pine Barrens is a heavily forested area located in the southern part of New Jersey. In other words, it is the perfect habitat for another legendary animal—the Jersey Devil.

Several New Jersey townships claim to be the birthplace of this cloven-hoofed, bat-winged fiend. They all have different stories related to its origin. One of the more common versions of the legend goes back to the 1730s. It is said that a woman named Mother Leeds gave birth to her thirteenth child one dark and stormy night. Unable to feed another mouth, the poor woman

The Pine Barrens region of southern New Jersey is thickly forested, making the area a perfect place for the Jersey Devil to hide.

cast the child out into the woods. Folklore says the child, enraged at being abandoned, turned into a fearsome, red-eyed, clawed creature with large, leathery wings, a forked tail, and horns. Legend has it that this beast then returned to its family and killed its mother, its drunken father, and many of its twelve siblings. Then, it flew up the chimney and into the wilds of the Pine Barrens.

Reports of the Jersey Devil spread throughout southern New Jersey in the 1800s. The beast was blamed for all sorts of disasters, including crop failures, droughts, polluted rivers, and the disappearance of numerous sheep and chickens. However, the biggest devil scare in recorded history occurred in 1909. In January of that year, citizens of many New Jersey towns, including Trenton, Mount Holly, and Woodbury, reported seeing the flying beast or finding its hoofprints in their yards or on their snowy rooftops. People in communities outside of southern New Jersey reported seeing the beast, too.

As more reports flooded in, people became too scared to leave their homes, and some factories and schools were forced to close. Unwilling to see this go on, members of the press set out to debunk the existence of the beast. In the months following the 1909 scare, several newspaper articles proclaimed the Jersey Devil to be a figment of people's imaginations. Faced with these reports, many people were no longer willing to believe in the devil. (At least, they wouldn't admit in public that they believed in it.) Angus Gillespie, an expert on New Jersey folklore, believes that at this point, the Jersey Devil started to lose some of its ability to terrify people.

However, that does not mean the Jersey Devil was never seen again. In more recent years, a few devil sightings have been reported in Vineland (1987), Winslow Township (1993), and Sayreville, New Jersey (1996). However, the New Jersey Pine Barrens is now much more developed than it used to be. The area that was once only dense woods is now peppered with wineries, golf courses, and neighborhoods full of cul-de-sacs and playgrounds. This makes it much more difficult for a devilish winged beast to hide and terrify the masses.

Approximately 500 miles (804.7 km) to the west of the Pine Barrens, in Point Pleasant, West Virginia, another terrifying winged creature once plagued local residents. In the thirteen-month period between November 1966 and December 1967, several people reported seeing a 6.5- to 7-foot (about 2 m) winged beast with glowing red eyes flying over the town. They estimated that it approached speeds of 100 miles (161 km) per hour. Some people thought the fearsome creature, dubbed "Mothman" by the press, was a warning of pending disaster.

On December 15, 1967, people's fears seemed to be realized when the Silver Bridge, which connected Point Pleasant with Kanauga, Ohio, suddenly collapsed during rush-hour traffic, killing forty-six people. After the bridge collapse, the Mothman was not seen again—until 2003. That year, a 12-foot (3.7-m) stainless-steel sculpture depicting him was erected in Mothman Park in downtown Point Pleasant.

On a trip to Mexico, a California man found this dried-up corpse. The strange being appears to have wings, two horns, and a tail. Could this be the remains of the Mothman?

Out in the Open

The Jersey Devil might still be able to hide in some parts of the Pine Barrens, but some flying cryptids have reportedly been seen out in the open. Imagine this: you are in the backyard playing on a nice summer day when, suddenly, two gigantic birds fly overhead. One of them swoops down, grabs you with its talons, and tries to fly away with you. Impossible? Ten-year-old Marlon Lowe of Lawndale, Illinois, probably thought so, too, until it happened to him one day in July 1977. Watching from a kitchen window, Marlon's mother quickly ran outside to save her son. Screaming at the dark-skinned, bald-headed creature, Marlon's mom successfully scared it away. It dropped the terrified boy and flew off.

In the following weeks, other residents of Illinois, as well as people in neighboring Indiana, also reported seeing large birds. Additional reports

International Cryptozoology Museum

The International Cryptozoology Museum is a one-of-a-kind museum filled with cryptid artifacts. Founded and curated by Loren Coleman, a leading cryptozoologist, the museum, located in Portland, Maine, opened its doors in 2003.

Coleman has been collecting cryptid specimens since 1960. The museum's artifacts include an 8-foot (2.4-m) model of Bigfoot produced by a Wisconsin taxidermist. There are also hair samples and more than one hundred footprints allegedly made by the big guy (or his relatives, including the Yowie and Yeti). The museum also contains artifacts dedicated to the Jersey Devil and West Virginia's Mothman. Along with the cryptid exhibits, Coleman also maintains a collection of well-known hoaxes, including a rubber Thunderbird, a jackalope, a furry trout, and a replica of P. T. Barnum's FeeJee mermaid. These objects, says Coleman, teach cryptozoologists to be careful about what they believe.

In addition to the International Cryptozoology Museum, there are a number of other museums dedicated to specific cryptids around the country, including the Bigfoot Museum in northern California; the Skunk Ape Research Headquarters in Ochopee, Florida; and the Mothman Museum in Point Pleasant, West Virginia, just to name a few.

poured in from as far south as Texas. Some eyewitnesses described the creature as a huge bat with large red eyes, leathery skin, and a gorillalike face.

It is possible that tales of these big birds are rooted in Native American myth. According to the legends of many Pacific Northwest and Great Plains tribes, an enormous bird, called the Thunderbird, makes thunder with the flap of its wings and flashes lightning from its eyes. While some tribes say the Thunderbird's favorite prey is the whale, others say the bird tends to snatch unsupervised children.

Loren Coleman, founder and curator of the International Cryptozoology Museum, holds a plaster skull made from fossils of a *Gigantopithecus*. Coleman is an expert on legendary primates.

Cryptozoologists believe that the Thunderbird may be linked to the pterodactyl, a prehistoric flying lizard. For a brief period in 2000, it looked as if they might have evidence for this. That year, a photograph emerged. It showed a group of men in Civil War uniforms standing over the dead body of a pterodactyl. But how could one of these winged lizards exist in the 1860s? Scientists believe that pterodactyls became extinct at the end of the Cretaceous period (220 to 65.5 million years ago) with all of the other dinosaurs.

It turns out that the photograph was actually a publicity stunt to promote the FOX TV program *Freakylinks*. The 22-foot (6.7-m) rubber "Thunderbird" shown in the photograph now resides in the International Cryptozoology Museum in Portland, Maine.

Chapter 5

Monsters, Beasts, and Demons Popping Up Everywhere!

Whether cryptids are real or not, these creepy creatures continue to fascinate people of all ages. They are featured in books. There are movies made about them. Numerous television shows endeavor to prove that they exist or debunk them entirely. Truly, if you are interested in monsters, beasts, and demons, American pop culture has them all.

Monsters at the Movies

The thrill of watching monsters on the big screen while safely munching on buttered popcorn in a movie theater just never seems to get old. In fact, many of the earliest films, made more than one hundred years ago, included various supernatural creatures. Myths, fables, and folklore featuring devils, demons, and monsters were the basis of many of these movies. Other films were adapted from horror classics of literature, such as Mary Shelley's *Frankenstein* and Bram Stoker's *Dracula*.

Some of these movies may have made their featured cryptids a bit too real in viewers' minds. For example, the year before the Green Clawed Beast grabbed Mrs. Darwin Johnson in Indiana, a similar creature appeared in the

The movie *Creature from the Black Lagoon* hit the screen a year before Indiana's Green Clawed Beast grabbed its victim. Was this just coincidence, or was there a connection?

horror movie *Creature from the Black Lagoon* (1954).

Did Johnson have a preconceived notion about a dangerous monster of the deep that could have influenced her perception of events? It's possible (although we do not know if Johnson ever actually saw *Creature from the Black Lagoon*).

Over the years, Bigfoot has starred in quite a few movies. Many films portray the big guy as a fearsome, vicious creature. But there are a few films, including *Harry and the Hendersons* (1987), *Bigfoot: The Unforgettable Encounter* (1994), and *Bigfoot: Friendship Can Get a Little Hairy* (2008), which characterize him as a gentler, kinder Sasquatch. The Mothman and numerous unnamed devils and demons have also been Hollywood stars at one time or another.

Watching monsters on the big screen is much more fun than running into them in real life.

Demons in the Den

The big screen is not the only place you are likely to encounter monsters, beasts, and demons. You can also turn on your television to see people present the latest eyewitness accounts and a wide variety

Josh Gates travels the planet investigating stories of supernatural occurrences. The show he hosts, *Destination Truth*, appears on the Syfy channel.

of physical evidence. Some TV shows invite scientists to try to determine if these unknown creatures really exist or not. In the four seasons of the History Channel's show *MonsterQuest*, for example, scientists have evaluated evidence for Bigfoot, Champ, Mothman, and many other legendary American creatures. *MonsterQuest* has since gone off the air, but it has been replaced with another show called *MysteryQuest* that examines supernatural phenomena.

The Syfy channel has a similar series called *Destination Truth*. In this show, American paranormal investigator Josh Gates and a group of fellow researchers travel the globe interviewing eyewitnesses and reviewing the evidence of supernatural incidents.

Another television series, *Lost Tapes*, airs on the Animal Planet channel. *Lost Tapes* takes a slightly different approach: it provides fictional encounters with a variety of cryptids, including Thunderbirds and the Jersey Devil. Older television shows of this kind, such as *Secrets of the Unknown* from the late 1980s, can still be found on videotape (and sometimes DVD) as well.

The popular science fiction series *The X-Files* ran for nine seasons between 1993 and 2002. The show featured two FBI agents (one a believer in the supernatural, the other a skeptic) who encountered various mythological creatures, including the Jersey Devil, a mysterious lake monster named Big Blue, and a human-bat hybrid creature that was never named.

Even the Cartoon Network has its own show about cryptozoology. It is called *The Secret Saturdays*, and it features a family of cryptozoologists. In the show, eleven-year-old Zak Saturday and his parents, Doc and Drew, attempt to keep the cryptids they track down a secret in order to protect them. As they travel the world, the Saturdays encounter cryptids such as the Louisiana Wookie (also called the Honey Island Swamp Monster), devil monkeys, lizard men, lake monsters, and the Swamp Ape.

Beasts in Books

Numerous books have been written about cryptids. These books range from nonfiction tomes describing the original legends to creative, fictional tales featuring the beasts.

The Committee for Skeptical Inquiry

The Committee for Skeptical Inquiry (CSI) is a nonprofit organization made up of scientists, academics, and science writers who use scientific methods to critically investigate supernatural phenomena. Some of their current and past members include Carl Sagan, Isaac Asimov, Francis Crick, and Richard Dawkins. The group's official journal, *The Skeptical Inquirer*, is published six times a year and includes scientific reviews of unusual sightings and experiences. Recent features include an analysis of a newly emerged video of Champ, an investigation of claims of demons in Connecticut, and a report on a search for vampire graves. Many of the articles can be read online at CSI's Web site, http://www.csicop.org.

The Cartoon Network's *The Secret Saturdays* has a companion book called *The Official Cryptid Field Guide*. The book details each of the show's cryptids, including its habitat, diet, and special powers. *Professor Horace, Cryptozoologist* by Kevin Scott Collier has a similar premise.

Another fictional offering, *The Dare Island Enigma* by Blake Templeton, features twelve-year-old Jesse and his friend, Lucas. The two friends discover a giant creature washed up on a North Carolina beach. In *Lost Days* by R. W. Ridley, fifteen-year-old Hayley Wilkes is determined to get to the bottom of her uncle's childhood encounter with a legendary creature. Thirteen-year-old twins, Grace and Marty, are the focus of *Cryptid Hunters* by Roland Smith. When their parents die, the twins are sent to live with an uncle who searches for unknown beasts.

Will Cryptids Survive?

Whether or not there really is a Bigfoot roaming the woods of the Pacific Northwest or a devilish creature lurking in New Jersey's Pine Barrens, such creatures live on in the American cultural landscape. People talk about them. They read about them. And they like to watch movies and television shows about them. Still, it is not clear that cryptids will survive.

One of the essential features of cryptids' way of life is separation from humans. When people spot them (and that does not happen all that often), monsters, beasts, and demons are invariably found in remote areas, such as dense forests, impenetrable swamps, or the depths of the ocean. However, in modern America, these places are rapidly disappearing.

In addition, pop culture may actually be threatening the believability of cryptids. When Bigfoot or the Jersey Devil is adopted by pop culture and souvenir shops sell bumper stickers, key chains, and sports pennants bearing the creature's name and likeness, it loses its ability to terrify people. Instead, the cryptid is transformed into something cute and cartoonlike. Such beasts then become something fun and interesting to talk about, rather than something that people truly believe in.

Many Americans today are less openminded than their ancestors when it comes to supernatural creatures. Now more than

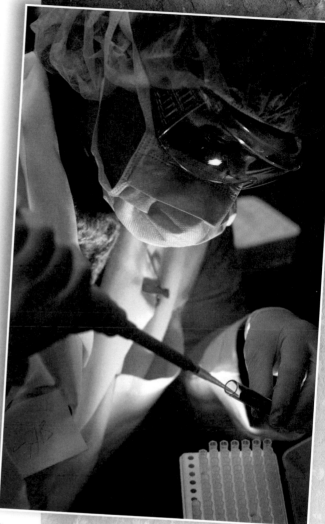

Today, people want definitive, scientific proof of the existence of cryptids.

ever, skeptics want proof, not fuzzy photographs and dubious video recordings, in order to believe that cryptids are real.

However, people with a strong belief in the supernatural can be equally hard to sway. With believers, scientists are in an unenviable position: they have to prove that something does not exist. Scientists are good at proving what does exist—a rock you can see, electricity you can feel and see do work—but proving that something does not exist is nearly impossible. All scientists can do is work with the physical evidence (things like fur, tissue, or bodies) that people claim have come from these creatures.

With DNA testing and the other scientific techniques available today, many mysteries can now be explained. Indeed, a large part of the job of science is to explain the natural world. But science can't explain everything—at least not immediately. What remains unexplained will always be susceptible to people's own unique explanations. Often, those explanations involve monsters, beasts, and demons.

Glossary

adapt To adjust to new conditions in order to survive.

albino An animal or human lacking in pigment.

anomaly Something different, abnormal, strange, or not easily classified.

biped An animal that walks upright on two legs.

bogeyman An imaginary evil creature often used by adults to frighten children into behaving.

contaminate To introduce foreign matter into a sample.

cryptid An unknown creature that may or may not exist.

cryptozoologist Someone who searches for evidence of cryptids.

debunk To show the falseness of a story, idea, statement, etc.

extinct Having no living members; having died out.

hominid A bipedal primate, including humans, of the Hominidae family.

hybrid The offspring of genetically dissimilar parents.

mutant An organism that shows new genetic characteristics due to changes in its DNA.

plaster cast A copy of a three-dimensional shape made by pouring liquid plaster of Paris into a mold.

plesiosaur A prehistoric, ocean-dwelling reptile with a flat body and paddle-like limbs that became extinct 220 to 65.5 million years ago.

pterodactyl A prehistoric flying lizard that became extinct 220 to 65.5 million years ago.

purport To claim to be or do a particular thing when this claim may not be true.

serpent A large snake.

skeptic A person who is slow to believe and quick to question; a doubter.

stride The distance covered in a complete step while walking.

tributary A river or stream that flows into a larger river or stream.

trident A spear with three prongs.

For Further Reading

Arnosky, Jim. *Monster Hunt: Exploring Mysterious Creatures with Jim Arnosky.* New York, NY: Hyperion, 2011.

Belle, Sebastian. *The Zak Files (The Secret Saturdays).* New York, NY: Golden Books, 2010.

Emmer, Rick. *Bigfoot: Fact or Fiction?* (Creature Scene Investigation). New York, NY: Chelsea House, 2010.

Emmer, Rick. *Loch Ness Monster: Fact or Fiction?* (Creature Scene Investigation). New York, NY: Chelsea House, 2010.

Everhart, Michael J. *Sea Monsters: Prehistoric Creatures of the Deep* (National Geographic Kids). Washington, DC: National Geographic, 2007.

Fairbanks, Randy. *The Weird Club: The Search for the Jersey Devil.* New York, NY: Sterling Publishing, 2007.

Gee, Joshua. *Encyclopedia Horrifica: The Terrifying Truth About Vampires, Ghosts, Monsters, and More.* New York, NY: Scholastic, 2007.

Halls, Kelly Milner, Rick Spears, and Roxyanne Young. *Tales of the Cryptids: Mysterious Creatures That May or May Not Exist.* Plain City, OH: Darby Creek Publishing, 2006.

Lewis, Brenda Ralph. *Prehistoric Creatures in the Sea & Sky* (Nature's Monsters: Dinosaurs). Milwaukee, WI: Gareth Stevens Publishing, 2007.

Matthews, Rupert. *Strange Animals* (QEB Unexplained). Mankato, MN: QEB Publishing, 2011.

McCormick, Lisa Wade. *Bigfoot: The Unsolved Mystery* (Blazers: Mysteries of Science). Mankato, MN: Capstone Press, 2009.

McNab, Chris. *Mythical Monsters: The Scariest Creatures from Legends, Books, and Movies.* New York, NY: Tangerine Press, 2006.

Olander, Johan. *A Field Guide to Monsters: Googly-Eyed Wart Floppers, Shadows-Casters, Toe-Eaters, and Other Creatures*. New York, NY: Marshall Cavendish, 2007.

Schulte, Mary. *The Dover Demon* (Mysterious Encounters). Detroit, MI: KidHaven Press, 2010.

Shealy, Dennis R. *The Official Cryptid Field Guide* (*The Secret Saturdays*). New York, NY: Random House, 2009.

Swanson, Diane. *Nibbling on Einstein's Brain: The Good, the Bad, and the Bogus in Science*. Rev. ed. Toronto, ON: Annick Press, 2009.

Wright, John D. *Cryptids and Other Creepy Creatures: The World of Unsolved Mysteries*. New York, NY: Tangerine Press, 2009.

Yomtov, Nelson. *Tracking Sea Monsters, Bigfoot, and Other Legendary Beasts* (Unexplained Phenomena). Mankato, MN: Capstone Press, 2011.

Bibliography

A&E Television Networks. "MonsterQuest: Sasquatch." History.com, 2011. Retrieved February 21, 2011 (http://www.history.com/shows/ monsterquest/interactives/monsterpedia-sasquatch#chasing-bigfoot).

Boese, Alex. "The Jackalope." Museum of Hoaxes, 2006. Retrieved February 21, 2011 (http://www.museumofhoaxes.com/tall-tales/ jackalope.html).

Britt, Robert Roy. "Supernatural Science: Why We Want to Believe." MSNBC.com, August 18, 2008. Retrieved February 21, 2011 (http://www.msnbc.msn.com/id/26268698).

Buhs, Joshua Blu. "First Chapter: 'Bigfoot: The Life and Times of a Legend.'" *New York Times*, June 5, 2009. Retrieved February 21, 2011 (http:// www.nytimes.com/2009/06/07/books/chapter-bigfoot.html).

Carroll, Robert T. "Charles Fort—The Skeptic's Dictionary." Skepdic.com, December 9, 2010. Retrieved February 21, 2011 (http://www .skepdic.com/fortean.html).

Coleman, Loren. *Mysterious America: The Ultimate Guide to the Nation's Weirdest Wonders, Strangest Spots, and Creepiest Creatures*. New York, NY: Paraview Pocket Books, 2007.

Coleman, Loren, and Jerome Clark. *Cryptozoology A to Z: The Encyclopedia of Loch Monsters, Sasquatch, Chupacabras, and Other Authentic Mysteries of Nature*. New York, NY: Simon & Schuster, 1999.

Discovery Communications, LLC. "Lost Tapes: Paranormal Creatures, Cryptozoology: Animal Planet." 2011. Retrieved February 21, 2011 (http://animal.discovery.com/tv/lost-tapes/meet-the-creatures).

Driscoll, John. "Birth of Bigfoot." Times-Standard Online, October 30, 2008. Retrieved February 21, 2011 (http://www.times-standard.com/ ci_10853838).

Epstein, Eric. "Jerseyana; Once Upon a Time, the New Jersey Devil Meant More Than Hockey." *New York Times*, April 26, 1998. Retrieved February 21, 2011 (http://www.nytimes.com/1998/04/26/nyregion/jerseyana-once-upon-a-time-the-new-jersey-devil-meant-more-than-hockey.html).

E. W. Scripps Co. "'Sea Monster' Revealed?" WPTV.com, January 11, 2010. Retrieved February 21, 2011 (http://www2.wptv.com/dpp/news/'Sea-monster'-revealed).

Kirby, Doug, Ken Smith, and Mike Wilkins. "International Cryptozoology Museum, Portland, Maine." RoadsideAmerica.com, 2011. Retrieved February 21, 2011 (http://www.roadsideamerica.com/story/24277).

Kirby, Doug, Ken Smith, and Mike Wilkins. "Mothman Statue, Point Pleasant, West Virginia." RoadsideAmerica.com, 2011. Retrieved February 21, 2011 (http://www.roadsideamerica.com/story/12036).

Nickell, Joe. "Tracking the Swamp Monsters." Committee for Skeptical Inquiry, August 2001. Retrieved February 21, 2011 (http://www.csicop.org/si/show/tracking_the_swamp_monsters).

Reuters. "California: Bigfoot Remains a Myth." *New York Times*, August 15, 2008. Retrieved February 21, 2011 (http://www.nytimes.com/2008/08/16/us/16brfs-BIGFOOTREMAI_BRF.html?_r=1).

Time, Inc. "Americana: The Champ of Champlain." Time.com, March 30, 1981. Retrieved February 21, 2011 (http://www.time.com/time/magazine/article/0,9171,922500,00.html).

Unknown Explorers. "Gloucester Sea Serpent." 2006. Retrieved February 21, 2011 (http://www.unknownexplorers.com/gloucesterseaserpent.php).

Viegas, Jennifer. "Bigfoot DNA Dubbed Scam, Believers Undaunted." Discovery News, August 15, 2008. Retrieved February 21, 2011 (http://dsc.discovery.com/news/2008/08/15/bigfoot-sasquatch-hoax.html).

Wagenseil, Paul. "'Montauk Monster' Has Hamptons in a Tizzy." FOX News Network, July 31, 2008. Retrieved February 21, 2011 (http://www.foxnews.com/story/0,2933,395294,00.html).

Index

About the Author

Kristi Lew is the author of more than forty science books for teachers and young people. Fascinated with science from a young age, she studied biochemistry and genetics in college. Before she started writing full-time, she worked in genetics laboratories and taught high school science. When she's not writing, she enjoys sailing with her husband aboard their small sailboat, *Proton*. As a scientist, Lew cannot help but be a bit of a skeptic. However, she tries to keep an open mind and is on the lookout for sea serpents and the Skunk Ape around her home in St. Petersburg, Florida.

Photo Credits